MW00900049

The "How to Not Make A Fool of Yourself" Guide

① The things that are worth their money are: shoes, umbrellas, bras, and bedding. It's okay to buy fewer of them as long as they're quality

② It's okay to ask a boy out. This isn't 1840 and you're not a helpless Southern belle.

Made in the USA
San Bernardino, CA
03 March 2017